Beauty Refracted

Also by Carol Moldaw

Poetry

Fiction

Beauty Refracted

Carol Moldaw

To Robin,

with admiration

and comradeship in poetry —

Carol

Salt Lake

1·17·19

Four Way Books

Tribeca

Library of Congress Cataloging-in-Publication Data

Names: Moldaw, Carol, author.
Title: Beauty refracted / Carol Moldaw.
Description: New York, NY : Four Way Books, [2018]
Identifiers: LCCN 2017029363 | ISBN 9781945588075 (softcover : acid-free paper)
Classification: LCC PS3563.O392 A6 2018 | DDC 811/.54--dc23
LC record available at https://lccn.loc.gov/2017029363

This book is manufactured in the United States of America and printed on acid-free paper.

Four Way Books is a not-for-profit literary press. We are grateful for the assistance
we receive from individual donors, public arts agencies, and private foundations.

PROUD MEMBER

[c|mp]

We are a proud member of the Community of Literary Magazines and Presses.

Distributed by University Press of New England
One Court Street, Lebanon, NH 03766

To Arthur, steadfast companion in life and art.

Contents

" . . . slipping in between
The beauty coming and the beauty gone."

Wordsworth, "Most Sweet It Is With Unuplifted Eyes"

I.

Of an Age

Less sleep but fewer tears.
Prayers pared down to tweets.
Desire scrubbed of sullenness.
A propensity for sweets—

but not truffles, truffles
I find too dense; chocolate-glazed
bacon, the idea of it, too strange.
Fads tempt less. A glass raised

in sentiment, more.
The fleet beauty of words
no longer encased, unsaid.
The glass in shards.

Loop: Pojoaque

A restless sleeper, the Pojoaque shifts
in its gravel bed and sighs, shrinks into itself,

secretes mud curls. I try to keep everything
I think in my head but each former thought

a new one displaces. By the time I'm home,
I forget them all. Owl guano drips down

the arroyo's side. On the mesa, small precipices,
out-juttings. Horsetail, tamarisk, grow

where they are blown, root in river sand—
also the cow hoof, the plexi camper shell.

Dream Loop #1

To suffer a loss of limb—
my right arm, my writing arm,
the foot I flex as I think—
to be crushed like a clove
under Krishna's juggernaut—
pressed to a verjuice
of tears—even on waking whole,
night's grief unstaunchable—
my father barefoot in snow.

A Measure

Did he hear—he raised
a brow—the prayers
Rabbi Marder led, arms
around his hospital bed?

Her chant transported
us at least: no one knows
(until it's too late
to do the living any good)

what the dying, let alone
the dead, hear. How
near they stay
before they really go.

Alert

Night sweats, sweat between my breasts;
the sheet slick; my mind
a mattress left out and pecked open,

stripped of its stuffing
by magpies battening their nest
high in the courtyard's cottonwood.

2 a.m., 3 a.m., 4,
Don't miss the bus, don't miss the bus,
my father talmudically warns

from beyond his freshly tamped grave
as an owl's twin search beams
exhume the dark. The nightly raid

begins with a series of hoots.
The sheets are soaked. The heart
I gave you, the one currently

confined in me, fibrillates
non-stop like a tin spoon
banged between iron bars,

self-celebration morphing
into panicked protest
in shadow of the owl's launch.

Cross Bearings

The wheels descend. We arrive
late: dazed, disheveled, with nothing
to declare. Once past customs
I have only to touch my mouth
to break another unspeakable rule.

For an immense but negotiable fee,
a man offers to drive us south,
but is *south* the way we want to go?
Pivoting, I spot the kiosk
with coupons for an official taxi.

From the window, conundrums
of unsheltered life mutely unspool.
In the flick-flack of roadside fires
I can just make out the moth wing
portion on which most survive.

I close my eyes. Let the scene dim.
Tomorrow we'll find amid traffic
a rotary shrine, a cacophonic hymn.
Tomorrow—a lingam of stacked tires,
a pilgrim's offering, pulverized brick.

Marginalia

1.

Abandoned buildings decompose
like compost in Delhi's fabled heat.

Traffic-stalled, transfixed, I watch
a man and woman clap and pound
brick against brick in an empty lot—

a mythic task: to pulverize by hand
the crumbling heap they squat atop.

Metronomic sun-chipped bangles
and a marigold-saffron sari persist

in afterimage as I inch away,
fixing the tableau: my marginalia,
the couple's unmitigated hours.

2.

Incense cones sizzling on iron griddles—cancer
remedies at "cut-throat" prices—encoded

outpourings of mint tea—corked vials of saffron
threads lining makeshift shelves—carved

sandalwood boxes stuffed with amber paste—
tiered flat baskets heaped with finely ground

umbers—cinnamon, turmeric, cardamom—
prayer's infinite anteroom—muted drama—

ticketed silks unsnapped—a fringe lit—barter's
coined clatter—the smell of burnt human hair—

3.

Not the scuttling of rats crossing our room
all night, nor the tub's rust-infested water,

nor the absence of moonlit midnight kisses
as we lay on our single pallets either side

of our daughter, and certainly not the raspy
swishing of palm leaves and cardboard

we wake to as early-morning street sweepers
clear debris, nor the sight by the guard box

of a barrel-chested man tilting a bucket
above his head so that cold water streams

down his face and rib-staves—none of this
can convince me that what I perceive isn't

self-induced, a dreamscape lacquered
on a city that seven substrata already litter.

Varanasi

In but not *of* this "city of light," where Shiva's
revelation's candled in every dying ear; where

every sadhu's a pilgrim, but not every pilgrim's
smeared in pyre-ash or daubed gold; shunted—

hustled—driver to guide—guide to boatman
to boatman's son—baksheesh to baksheesh—

until, like contraband, our point of origin's
untraceable—pulled through the packed-dirt

mud-pocked streets—the one drab thread
in an oversaturated whirling blur

of noise-blasted, stink-infused throbbing color—
siphoned off at the top of Panchganga Ghat

to negotiate the steps, the cripples, the slippery
mat-haired children who swarm us to sell

marigold petals, bits of candle wax we'll light—
with matches they also sell—an offering

we set afloat from the skiff, see it now,
gently bobbing, the oarsman bringing it in.

*

Setting my lit candle-bit adrift on a leaf raft,
careful not to let my fingers graze

the Ganges' toxic holy water, water said
to flow directly from Shiva's matted hair,

I follow my teardrop flame down the current
until it joins the other flickering lights,

the river's reflection doubling each—the way,
putting this to words, I reflect, amplify,

contrive—my father's word—a double
of the flickering prayer I murmured for him

and set, bepetalled, adrift to join the nebula
of little flames the current kept at a spin;

a prayer uttered despite knowing that he—
fastidious in his disbelief—would have hated

this city of churning filth and faith,
the two swirling together, inextricably

bound like two knots of putty melded
and softened in a sadhu's soil-stained hand.

*

Now, under a low-lying Virginia sky
that mutes the luster of blossoming trees

as if to show off crab apple, dogwood,
redbud, cherry in full unmitigated sun

would be too much glory to reveal—
under this subtle light that lets time slip

its rigid demarcations supply as a cat
that slithers between fence slats to hunt

old haunts, three years on, the spiking fires
of the cremation ghat come into view

as the oarsman rows as close as allowed,
skirring the dark waters to keep us in place

with other tourist skiffs. "No photographs,"
he warns. Binoculars aimed and focused,

I can see, as little pops ignite, the still intact
pattern of threads on a charred shroud,

can see a lolling, swollen foot snap and fall,
my father's Hermès tie, his best suit—

removed or not, under the winding cloth,
I never thought to ask; can see mourners

who, just as they milled about my mother's
candle-lit living room, circle the pyre,

language's light felicity linking Shiva the god
to shiva, the designated period of grief,

the *i* in each like flames at a different tilt,
so that when I overhear in inflected English

a nearby boatman telling passengers
the mourners are doing everything wrong—

wrong the direction of the body and wrong
the direction mourners circle as they chant,

the chant wrong—and the way the oxygen
mask he had stopped fighting against muzzled

his last thoughts so that they resounded only
in the hold of his own head, revelations

pooling to overflow the lip of the snail shell
whorl of his dying ear—the marigold petals

whirling downriver resolve themselves at last
into apple blossoms on a rain-soaked lawn.

At the Pond

Light the pond reflects
is both diffused and absorbed:
today the surface

enshrouded in close-knit clouds
no bass no trout nor I breach.

*

Five duck eggs nested
in arrow grass. At my footfall,
the mother flies up.

Friends scatter. With you gone,
who will know me anymore?

*

Absence a presence
at first: as if, like water
let loose, the spirit

unembodied flows outward
into those of us closest.

*

As in an Escher,
the negative space, the space
absented by you,

stared at intently, pops out,
dominating the picture

until we adjust
and the black cutout recedes,
leaving a new take

on you, a structural plane
sharply incorporeal.

*

It's late May again.
Great stands of yellow iris
emblazon the pond.

Last year, I missed their flourish—
herald now of your Yahrzeit.

II.

Three Fascinations

1.

—to wake to an alarm
of kisses, a slow
fastening embrace, not
the standard issue
cold compress pillow.

2.

It's not—I shrieked
—*not business as usual.*
The words, as the car
climbed, exhilarated:
a rise each iteration,
shriller than the last,
increased until, as if
fastened in their grip,
the grip of mourning,
I could claim to be
lifted above the drear
din of the mundane.

3.

Rifts, elisions, occult
desires, concrete
regrets: sorted not
unlike laundry into day-piles
and night; dream and
day-dream; the unattained,
the unattainable; into ". . . of
what's difficult" " . . . to
a dying animal"; into what,
of that, can be goaded,
bleating, into words.

Loop: Roanoke

Daily, I traipse the Hollins Loop:
from Duchouquet
you can start up Faculty Row
and visit the stables
or go the other way, up
a tractor path in the grass
to the founders' cemetery. One day
David showed me an even smaller path
that led past a caved-in house:
doorframe in splinters, glassless
windows, the roof collapsed,
everything faintly, peelingly, blue.
Past the house, the path led
the back way to a neighborhood
suburban and well-kempt,
nothing to distinguish it except
it had once been, he said, all black.
I could have grown up there.
Scarlet peonies bloom at the same time
ours do, a big stand of them, against
the theatre. It makes me shiver
with missing home. At the creek
we looked for ducks. I liked

the horses at dusk, the tulips
above the president's house.
I'm not sure what I felt
about the cemetery. If only
I'd hoisted myself up
on the boundary wall and balanced
on that stark divide
like a feckless fifteen-year-old
or leaned a long time against
a headstone's narrow headboard,
then surely I would know.

Dew Point

From one I learn what robotripping is;
from another, the names of clouds:

diamond dust, sundog, fallstreak hole,
cloudbow, fogbow, crepuscular ray.

Despite his anchor-pierced clavicle,
the languorous boy sprawled across

a poem's quilt needs no explication,
and I've already googled Quetiapine

to make sense of rimed nipple crust—
but what, I'm forced to ask outright,

is a *tramp stamp?* There's stifled laughter
until, with a self-conscious candor

I knew once in myself, an arch girl
gets up from the conference table,

pirouettes on an Ugg and crouches
to expose above tattered low-rise jeans

and spanning her iliac crest, a tatted set
of lilac fairy wings, as innocent as she.

Loop: Jacona Road

—Not me, but the moment
upon me as I turn
down our road, almost home:
above and beyond
the Jemez, hoofprint clouds
and then, before the sun's gone down,
rising behind a neighbor's stand
of furled-in elms
and glancing across our drive,
the moon's impeccable rising.

Sibylline Syllables

Omens women
moan, monotone
moonstone,

tuned—cured
carved, scarred,
scorched, blurred,

blued, bled—
to fortune's forked
torturing tines.

A Leaf's Gravity

A man hired by the man who dredged the pond
documented twenty-six kinds of birds
at the southern bend of the Pojoaque River
early one April morning. Like the autistic girl
who glided up to you in a tot pool
when your daughter was small, and peered at you
unseeing, reminding you, against your will,
or perhaps it was against your better judgment,
of a blind fish—as you mull over ways
to incorporate the subcontractor's list
into a poem, you stare blankly,
first at the page, then out the window.
All month you've been watching flurries of leaves
catch in the sunlight as they flutter down.
Weighing "the gravity of a leaf" against
"a leaf's gravity," you don't notice the drift
of your mind until, as in a newscast recap,
the rabbit is already writhing, tossed
from the wheels of the car ahead.
As before, you're glad you aren't the driver,
but angry too, because you'd seen the rabbit—
if you'd been in front you could have swerved
and saved it. Whether impotent anger

or relief came first, you're not sure, and which
emotion is truer—stronger—you also can't say.
Even now, you wish you'd stopped to bury it,
the way you buried your daughter's Siamese kitten,
mauled by the dogs next door. Small calamities,
you know, compared to the world's, some
of which you register before you glide away.

The Fate of the Painting Is Their Fate

A man steadies a balance
while a woman weighs

their gold. Brushstroked in,
burnished, embodying

the canvas as the canvas
embodies them, they are

not free to flee its looting
or history's gilded frame.

Myodesopsia

What would he make of us now, he who despised
getting his inexplicably pianist-fine hands soiled?

The perspective of that *he* doesn't exist anymore.

On the curved scrim of my retina, vitreous floaters
bob and sway in silhouette, like shadow puppets—

I want to swat them off the darkened stage
but they persist, gnat-like, just out of reach.

*

When his gold-rimmed watch vanished off my wrist,
two years to the day, I panicked, as if the soul

had been encoded on it, illiquid but transferable.
Later, when it reappeared, I locked it in a drawer.

All synopsis or isolated moment, memory distils
time into meaning, but pickles what it enshrines.

*

Where a horse now leans against bent fence posts
and mangled wire, one night a pickup crashed

and rolled. The driver died, the truck got towed.
For months we encountered his scattered effects:

house keys clipped to a mud-caked carabiner;
tape-wrapped pliers; splintered CDs; rabbit's foot

still soft as the field's cerulean-velvet wild iris
that grow in clusters, to wither in a day or two.

I think of him, yet a stranger, when I use the pliers.

*

Who is it lays out the deliberate arrangement
of sheep hooves and hides we find some Easters

at the arroyo's mouth? And who would position
a cushionless couch, stained and slashed, aslant

the river as if to lounge and watch it like TV
on exposed and rusted coils? Or leave to its stink

an open-eyed, jaggedly cut deer head
in the wheel-rutted off-road? What transactions

do men conduct through rolled-down windows,
engines running? Bullet casings, paper targets

tacked to the crumbling mesa, amber empties
propped on sandstone ledges, shattered in the grit.

When I see fresh mud tracks, I leash the dog, turn back.

*

In spring, backhoes haul dirt along the still dry bed
and berms are tamped and beveled to train

the seasonal water along newly wedged runnels,
but when the separate currents swell beyond their banks

to join in one large braided flow, uprooted saplings
get swept downstream along with rope-string mop heads.

Ever since the dump fees rose, more diapers,
condoms, Tampax, fridges, washing machines.

*

Trade routes, rivers, the routes of the dead.

Gravestones, the paving stones: chiseled names
and dates worn, effaced by the brunt of wheels.

For a while I watch the flecks in my eye as if sighting
on the horizon spinner dolphins frolicking.

Then I try to ignore them. My father too dives
unpredictably in and out of focus, sometimes hidden,

sometimes sharpened, by an impervious divide.
That dark pond in the grass?—A cottonwood's shadow.

Loop: The Barrancas

Somewhere inside poems written
to avoid unwritable ones
are wisps of what I turned from.
If not inside, then suspended,
like a full moon at 6 a.m., drained
of color in a rust ring of cloud.

I like to time things to the minute
but having fifteen minutes leeway
is more reliable, allows for time
spent watching the puff and dissolve
of contrails fat as SUV tracks
in the arroyo's impressionable sand.

To register to scale what's intangible,
I take the ridge to where the trail
tapers off and the view expands,
range after range, our own house,
small from here, one among many,
just past the curve of silver poplars.

As Far as I Can Tell

A lidless idleness designed to mesmerize,
out of which hesitancy and reluctance

give way to calibrations minute but not
insignificant, day in, day out, rocked

by the tidal bed the shell it's attached to
is attached to, complacent in its mantle

of unconscious soft tissue, it grows radially
as if from a sound wave's central ping

or like a breath-fired ball of molten glass.
The irritant of particularity's the seed

that starts the exacting earnest venture,
the salt inside consequent iridescence.

III.

Conundrum

for N.R.

Pear-shaped and hanging piñata-like
from the branch of a fruiting pear tree,
the paper wasp nest—once I saw it

for what it was—became an emblem
for things not being what they seem,
and quick-as-a-blink hard-to-shake

associations. Even the sun, remember,
has cold spots and, more apt, sweet spots
on fruit, where the sugar's concentrated,

look like bumpy blemishes, fatal flaws.
Maybe the mind isn't a sieve after all,
I thought, but a geode, whose scraped

casing conceals mineralized reserves:
chalcedony, amethyst, quartz. Or wasps.
I was eyeing the nest again, its flaking

marbled gray concentric papier-mâché
layers as thin as Saturn's rock-and-ice rings.
Our rupture had been a wreckage so total

as to shutter any memory of what exactly
had been wrecked. Only now, years later,
a glimmer: an eclipsed sun's black pearl.

For a Lost Fragment

for C. H.

It's a definite lack, being landlocked, bay-and-ocean-less:
I envy you the lapping ferry, especially on your way home,
as you face the receding city to catch sunset's neon sprawl.

Life itself can feel like a sprawl these days, but I'm grateful
emotions no longer roil heedlessly inside me, unchecked
as the flash flood that yesterday surged through the Pojoaque,

lifting it beyond its sand-grit bed and churning up a swill
of watered-down mud. When we were young, on the coast
of Spain, it was all I could do to keep my agitations down.

Who knew how to admit to the furious flurry caged inside?
At the overpass, a long line of cars—it looked like a pileup—
had emptied out to spectate the tumult moiling below.

To see the swollen river up close, once home I put on
waders and crossed our field, flooded only in pockets
until near the back V-gate, where suddenly the water rose

knee-high with a pushing force and a continuous roar
like a full-on stampede—the escaped river trampling its bed,
flattening cottonwood, salt cedar, Russian olive, in its wake.

Submerged like a floodplain, the past's reshaped by brush
and bracken being swept downstream, by the water that,
subsided, reveals corrective contours, blank spaces, scraps

missing, regretted, newly understood. I wish I still had
that unfinished love poem I scrawled in a long-lost ledger.
As if it could ferry us back, redirect one moment's course.

On the Way to the Acupuncturist

In the wrong lane, the slow one—
I do what I have to, to get out.
It takes awhile, and the dynamics
of the lanes shift. Shift again.
Nineteen minutes to get there.

Cars pass me, but why do I care:
I still have time. It's being
behind the curve that rankles—
I want to catch the traffic lights'
green wave, latch onto the tailwind.

Confessional

Red tinsel wrapped around a roadside cross
glints in the sun like a cop's strobe bar,
then recedes into the drive's unbroken trance.

Power lines Xacto-knife the sky.
Pasted and scraped, a billboard's pastel
palimpsest, photographed in raking light.

Our eyes locked on the road, stories unpeel
in the rental car's souped-up and streamlined
confession box. Stripped of penance and shame,

some of what we say exhaust drowns out,
some's keenly heard. Above sandstone cliffs,
low-level clouds mop up the sun's spillover—

or is that the sun dabbing at the clouds'
sniffed-back tears? Tell me a bizzaro factoid
that implicates yourself. See if I swerve.

The Nature of Desire

To fulminate, to go on a tear,
because what's wanted

is forbidden—not that I have,
but the idea of it: others do

and I can imagine it, imagine
it getting to that point. The idea

excites me, a state I can refuse
to entertain and thus prolong.

Metrics

Though the earnestness of artists bores me
as do admonitions in art,

I admit I begrudge certain words
for worming their way into my poems.

Too bad I can't hang up on them,
as on a robocall or marketing survey.

A word shouldn't diminish the thing it names.
Who would want to "engage in foreplay"?

Fellatio's at least a word worth mouthing.
I also notice I've gotten more attentive, more

painstaking, regarding my likes and dislikes
and less bemused by those of others.

"Does the Dalai Lama fly coach?"
the dowager asks the table, a flirty laugh

underscoring her point: one-up on him
and, though a widow, nobody's fool.

Sunday Afternoons

Sundays, nobody emails.
Sunlight turns the curtains puce.

We pull the chaise from the wall
to face the horseshoe fire

and say only what we mean.
I see eyes in the grains

of a ceiling beam, ghost-like
bodies wafting in the saw-cut.

Oiled, my feet climb
then slip from your thighs.

Innocence

Your number was 120; the lottery got to 90.
I would have gone to Canada, you said, candlelight
pocking the smooth alabaster of your chest.

Outside the window, a whiplashing of leaves.
My relief, even so many years beyond,
is sharp, visceral, laced with a stubborn will.

Hail is all I want to know of shrapnel,
camisoles of camouflage. Angling two fingers
up and down the speed bumps of your ribs,

like a skier taking moguls, I try not to
imagine you young, as perishable
and unmarked then as our nephews now . . .

Stopped in My Tracks En Route

Not for my ivory, woolens, amber, glass,
or the two torque-torsoed acrobats
whose limbs entwine, an ever-spinning globe;
not for ostrich eggs or my agate-eyed warhorse,
his silver-bezelled saddle; nor the caravan
itself, its frill of arabesques red-gold
under mud crackle. No: my turban burned,
my breast-binding cummerbund unwound,
the hinged row of hooks popped open,
the pins damming my hair, the bedding,
your bolt of molten silk, unrolled,
alabaster white, jade-smooth, jade-hard.

Love Song

Never one
to rim a room with candles,

I like to lounge
semi-clothed in seeming

indifference
as you make the round,

little pots of flame
planted along your path.

Remember how, no matter what,
you used to lunge for me?

Now you await a signal
to part the curtain

of my hair, wait
with stung patience

for me
to write this down.

Young Love

Always short a card, nostalgia
lays out its dog-eared deck
in a horseshoe spread, chooses
from the apex an iconic image:
her head in his lap, his hand
ruffling her hair, the two of them
dreamy midday, as if sleep were
the greater part of consciousness.
Cigarettes balanced on the rim
of a wrought iron table dangle
ash; for years they live
in the aura of inevitability
they radiate, in love
with a tautological logic:
It was. It had to be. Hindsight,
with its stacked deck, knows
what happens next
and so no doubt do you—
but they themselves, they,
poor lambkins, are blindsided.

Mutable Lies

The lie (that) you would forget.

The lie you spend your life remembering.

The lie that love endures.

The lie that love is passing.

The lie you are too blind to see.

The lie for your own good.

The lie you know best.

The lie I lie back to.

Since Then

Outside the high windows of what was once
our kitchen—before that, a weaver's room—now a study—
breeze-bent lilacs continue to wave and sway;

the weeping willow grazes buffalo grass;
copper roses blaze and extinguish,
blaze and extinguish and blaze . . .

but the peacock that appeared one afternoon
strutting up and down the back garden's brick path
hasn't been seen again, and was not—

unlike the five tawny owlets
perched for weeks on a beam of the kitchen *portal*—
digitally photographed, turned into a screen saver.

Almost everything's been put on automatic pay
but on some cloudless nights
I find my doormat's openwork rubber

enstarred with a cellophane sheen—
the moon's monthly bill,
still in his name.

Loop: Marfa

A fence constructed of windmill
blades near two bladeless windmills;

a herd of wild antelope grazing
pasture cordoned off for cows . . .

the antelope, guarding their hooves,
do the limbo rather than leap barbed wire.

Young, I wanted love to cocoon me.
Today I ask of it: *make me considered*

and canny as the swift antelope;
resourceful, a refashioner of windmills.

IV.

Dream Loop #2

The way inmates and their families
hold palms up to opposite sides of glass—
even without touch, seeing you comforts.
We, the imprisoned; you, free to go,
your sentence commuted, the terms no longer
a source of agony, tedium, despair, joy, hope
or spite. All crimes absolved, death
its own rehabilitation. This time the setting
is a crowded beach, a grilled burger
in your hand. Are you all of nineteen?
Or thirty-five, an image from childhood.
Joy radiates out of your eyes.
I too am elated, though with no chance
to discuss the dilemmas that vex me—
your detachment not unloving or cold
but a state few of us living attain.

Corrective

for Sue

They trained us well, in some regards:
not to settle in shabby neighborhoods;
always to call when we travel, and call
on our return; never to stray far or, at least,
if going far, not to stay away too long;
to remember and celebrate with them
their birthdays and anniversaries as they
invariably remembered to celebrate ours.
Quick learners, we soon figured out
how not to disappoint and how not
to arouse suspicion or undue angst:
our living arrangements conventional,
our reported behavior beyond reproach—
until, eventually, our lives became our own.

Beauty, Refracted

"Every dark thing one falls into can be called an initiation"
The Feminine in Fairytales, Marie-Louise von Franz

Like a storybook girl emerged from the split
pit of a peach, or one miraculously drawn up

from the murky depths of a wishing well,
her origins are unknown, except to those

who placed her where she would be found
and thus lost the ability to track her.

If you only see someone before your eyes
have learned to focus, have you really seen

that person?—She knows her mother
inside out, but only from the inside out:

the face she sees is a blank: it is *her* face.
The faces that aren't blank aren't hers.

*

To be named Beauty, specifically Beauty
in the flowering form of a winter lotus;

to be transplanted, shifted from the crib
of one continent to the hip of another,

the pitch and heave of infancy a sleep
like an oceanic voyage you wake from

far from where you started, the memory
of what and who were left behind opaque

as stirred mud, as pond muck that feeds
the sacred flower's submerged roots.

To find your name a neologism
coined expressly for you, to be seen

from infancy as embodying an imaginary
seasonal varietal of an aquatic known

to revive and germinate after a stasis
suspended over a thousand years:

your given name a navigational star
by which you learn to track cosmic seas.

*

For nights on end, on a cable
of finger-knit pink yarn
looped around a ceiling beam,
Donk, the compact donkey,
hangs suspended, her bed his
safety net. All the Bunny World
is assembled to watch: even
the other performers watch.
The troupe's called Cirque du Lune.
Cornelia, the pink unicorn,
stars, romantic and lithe
as the trapeze artist in Old Maid.
Her straddle-climb up the silks
and free-fall drop are perfect.

Donk can't help but heap
scorn on everyone, slighting
and taunting even his friends:
Moo-Cow, troubadour Buddha,
and dear Loopy, the tender lion
whose symbol's an endlessly looping
lemniscate, as his name implies.
In the Bunny World, we all live

on the same block; friends own
neighboring houses. A street map
to the stars, two restaurants,
a general store and a gym
can be found gridded out
in a spiral bound notebook.

No amount of money can buy
a cloud, so in the Bunny World
there is no money, no commerce.
No dating either, at first, though
Briar Rose, the frolicking mare,
pines for Phoebus, who lost an eye
in battle and, chivalrous lion
that he is, pretends not to notice.
Whose idea was it to introduce
the troupe to spin-the-bottle?
—Their personalities a mash-up
of psyches, free-associative patter,
riffed-on pratfall, put-down,
peacemaking, each night refines.

*

Planetary perturbations, hormonal
insurrections: when Beauty's finger's

pricked on Maya's spinning wheel,
she's felled, locked in the keep

of childhood, the household held
to a standstill. Only love mitigates

the spell. Pollen velvets the sills;
board games crowd the kitchen table.

The last bit of green sparkle chipped
off her nails, she sorts through cards,

seeking the peppermint pass of Queen
Frostine, old ally, to airlift her up.

*

No confirmed observations have been made
of the Oort Cloud where she perambulates

light years from the sun. Demagnetized, she's lost
her bearings: impassable barrier—though unlocked—

the door on which she bangs, her wail
a hard-charging squad of sirens, a comet's tail

trawling the far cosmos for a sign. The trail's
evaporated. The face she yearns for—a lost piece

of the puzzle that is herself—has fallen through
the flooring, down the crack of a synaptic cleft.

*

At first Beauty thought
Briar Rose's mooning
over DaVinci, a Morgan
Beauty had begun riding
once a week at the barn,
was just a ploy to get
Phoebus's attention back,
if she'd ever even had it.

Her voice, already high,
pitched up as she pled
to be allowed in the barn
for a "reunion" played
and perfected on the rug:
the tale of how, as colts,
they had romped in a field
swooningly punctuated.

With no eligible stallions
to assail, Briar Rose moped
in cast-off elbow-length
white satin dress-up gloves
that sagged at her knees,

all the while eyeing Shawny,
the stocky rocking horse,
and now and again pawing

the air in front of Poley,
the gigantic but benign
polar bear—both courtiers
off limits to all but Beauty,
whose fierce reign kept
everyone prancing in place,
the troupe's social order
as prescribed as dressage.

*

When Beauty, slip-knotted to a flimsy rope,
begins her descent, rappelling down, I don't think

about the large array of girls who disappear
from reality's surface, trapped in the unconscious—

of the opening the meadow made for Koré,
or Alice, swilled down a rabbit hole's throat.

When into the full-length curtain's smothering swaddle
she flings herself like an amped-up moth rushing

to collide with a fatal beam of light, and when,
with every thrash and twirl, the curtain's corset

tightens its stays, I don't—who on earth would?—
have the presence of mind, the detachment, the faith,

to take heart in how poor Snow White survived
the lace-up bodice her stepmother devised

to squeeze her lung-sponges dry, survived
the flesh-harrowing comb, the poisonous bite.

What can we, the petrified, do, except stand
guard impassively until the paroxysm breaks,

then coax her out like a kitten, flex her claws
free of the netting, keep the curtains tied.

*

A hundred days—a hundred years—asleep
in the same bed, all three of us at first,

crammed into our allotted slots: Beauty,
given how much she flails, put on one side,

mine—as the mother-flank—the one chosen.
The father can't ever be center, he is male

and must, within his given role, maintain
an ideal ratio between closeness and distance.

Beside her, I begin to supplicate, soothe,
cajole, fuss, and fume—careful not to tease,

as I lead her back to her own bed, her nest
of plumped pillows. Our rituals evolve

over time: like Scheherazade's, our days
and nights of storytelling as we play,

chatter, fight, and sleep with the animals
who crowd the bed's ready-made stage set.

Beauty had always said she wouldn't date
until her hundred-and-fiftieth birthday

but one night whittled that down to fifteen,
a revision tantamount to taking an axe

to the thicket of brambles separating her
from her yet-to-be-awakened self.

*

—Briar Rose started a school—became a scold—tried to enforce a code

of conduct no one could hold to—half the troupe ducked out, cut class—

Cornelia threw a hissy fit—egged on Donk to graffiti the cafeteria with fat

flowers—put up her hooved dukes—the sisters fought to a standoff—

Loopy called for a *truss*—meaning a *truce*—but no one trusted that it would

last past Moo Cow's ballad at Beauty's bedtime—the entire troupe piled up

to hear his tropes—heroic tales of the bad times—when Phoebus shed blood

defending them, lost an eye—collective sigh—nervous laugh—then one

by one they crept—to kiss Beauty before—she kicks them to the floor—

*

She wanted to refuse time's shape-shifting
imperatives, so night after night wore

the same panda-print purple night shift
until its neck and armholes began to pinch,

the hem rapidly inching up like bamboo—
though of course it was she, not it, that grew

in secret weed-like sleep-sprints we ignored
until keeping herself intact no longer meant

staying the same. When she abruptly skidded
to a screeching halt, her heels making wheelies

in the dirt, how unexpected was it? A part
of her apparently knew that other parts

couldn't catch up unless she stopped outright
or willy-nilly went back to fetch them.

*

When Beauty wakes, the generation of squirrels
whose every name she lovingly handpicked

as they scampered across her path, has given way,
replaced by more anonymous offspring.

Corolla-like, her girlish hips have flared;
the last of her milk teeth has been pushed out;

only she is allowed to brush her long thick hair:
slowly, yet all at once, is how Beauty woke.

If in most ways the world remained the same—
the earth still spinning atilt its daily axis

as it orbits the sun and the moon orbits it,
our deadly fuels, our feuds and constant perils—

Beauty's inner compass has been reset.
Who can say how? She woke, not to a kiss

but to herself, and once that sealed-off sleep
has slipped away, it dream-like stays forgotten.

Loop: Arroyo Grande

Barbed wire proves to be tumbleweed.
March 25th: he would have been 85.
Clouds amass, but warm spring ones.

Along the arroyo's eroded sides, roots
hang exposed to the air, as if epiphytic.

Ahead, Miranda snaps at the heels of two
helmeted men dismounting dirt bikes
where the sand's collapsed in a heap.

Though secretly pleased, I rebuke her
until 502 traffic supplants their revving.

Then, in the brush, wind, the near crackle
of paws and feet on leaves, dry grasses.
At some point all this will blur into "walk,"

into "sheep pelt not seen on the way out,"
into "wind, no rain." Outside the gate,

on the road, our daughter, 12, on a bike,
having lately learned to ride, no thanks to us.
At 55, I relish being carnate more now,

consider each moment a last hurrah
before first slips delight, then embodiment.

Kakapa Bay

As if at the near edge
of an expanse of blue chemise,
froth scallops the lava
collar bone of a rock point.

Past the slate roofline
of the house below us,
the air is all fan snap,
palms batting off wind.

Across the water, behind
a light haze, Haleakalā
visible atop Maui. There,
we're situated amid a horizon

one part of my mind rests on
while another part scans
itself for landmines
sensitive enough to detonate

even under the gingerly
tread of these bucolics.
Mulling over every word,
strip-searching sighs, I

follow the leads I let drop,
keep the assurances I make,
the bribes offered in exchange
for any promising morsel.

Crab eyes shrimp eyes string
of pearls. The water boils away.
The tea steeps. I work past dark,
husband, daughter, fast asleep.

Acknowledgments

Grateful acknowledgment is made to the editors of the following journals and anthologies in which these poems first appeared, sometimes in a slightly different form or under a different title:

AGNI; The Album; Alhambra Poetry Calendar, 2013; Chokecherries: 20 Years Anniversary Edition; Chronicle for Higher Education; Construction Magazine; Denver Quarterly; FIELD; Green Mountains Review; Harvard Review; Hollins Critic; Malpaís Review; Massachusetts Review; Narrative; The New Yorker; Platte Valley Review; Ploughshares; Plume; The Plume Anthology of Poetry, 2012; The Plume Anthology of Poetry, 2013; The Plume Anthology of Poetry, 2014; Poet Lore; PoetsArtists; Sou'wester; The Taos Journal of Poetry and Art; and *Vallum.*

With thanks to Jeffrey Harrison, Dana Levin, Martha Collins, Jim Moore, Cathy Hankla, Miriam Sagan, Peter Mattair and, always, Arthur Sze, for their support and readings of these poems at different stages.

Carol Moldaw has published six books of poetry. She has also published one novel, *The Widening. The Lightning Field* won The 2002 FIELD Prize and a volume of selected poems, *So Late, So Soon,* was published in 2010. A recipient of an NEA Fellowship, a Pushcart Prize and A Lannan Foundation Marfa Writers Residency, her work has been translated into Turkish, Chinese, and Portuguese. She has published poems in *The New Yorker, The New Republic, Paris Review, AGNI, FIELD* and many other magazines and anthologies, including *Western Wind: An Introduction to Poetry*, and *Under 35: A New Generation of American Poets.* From 2005-2008 Moldaw was on the faculty of Stonecoast, the University of Southern Maine's low-residency M.F.A. program, and she has conducted residencies at the Vermont Studio Center, taught at the College of Santa Fe and in the MFA program at Naropa University. In the spring of 2011 she served as the Louis D. Rubin, Jr., Writer-in-Residence at Hollins University. She lives in Santa Fe, New Mexico, with her husband, Arthur Sze, and their daughter.

Publication of this book was made possible by grants and donations. We are also grateful to those individuals who participated in our 2017 Build a Book Program. They are:

Anonymous (6), Evan Archer, Sally Ball, Jan Bender-Zanoni, Zeke Berman, Kristina Bicher, Laurel Blossom, Carol Blum, Betsy Bonner, Mary Brancaccio, Lee Briccetti, Deirdre Brill, Anthony Cappo, Carla & Steven Carlson, Caroline Carlson, Stephanie Chang, Tina Chang, Liza Charlesworth, Maxwell Dana, Machi Davis, Marjorie Deninger, Lukas Fauset, Monica Ferrell, Emily Flitter, Jennifer Franklin, Martha Webster & Robert Fuentes, Chuck Gillett, Dorothy Goldman, Dr. Lauri Grossman, Naomi Guttman & Jonathan Mead, Steven Haas, Mary Heilner, Hermann Hesse, Deming Holleran, Nathaniel Hutner, Janet Jackson, Christopher Kempf, David Lee, Jen Levitt, Howard Levy, Owen Lewis, Paul Lisicky, Sara London & Dean Albarelli, David Long, Katie Longofono, Cynthia Lowen, Ralph & Mary Ann Lowen, Donna Masini, Louise Mathias, Catherine McArthur, Nathan McClain, Gregory McDonald, Britt Melewski, Kamilah Moon, Carolyn Murdoch, Rebecca & Daniel Okrent, Tracey Orick, Zachary Pace, Gregory Pardlo, Allyson Paty, Marcia & Chris Pelletiere, Taylor Pitts, Eileen Pollack, Barbara Preminger, Kevin Prufer, Vinode Ramgopal, Martha Rhodes, Roni & Richard Schotter, Peter & Jill Schireson, Soraya Shalforoosh, Peggy Shinner, James Snyder & Krista Fragos, Megan Staffel, Alice St. Claire-Long, Robin Taylor, Marjorie & Lew Tesser, Boris Thomas, Judith Thurman, Susan Walton, Calvin Wei, Abby Wender, Bill Wenthe, Allison Benis White, Elizabeth Whittlesey, Hao Wu, Monica Youn, and Leah Zander.